ASS! It means "DONKEY"
and a lot of other things

Text and Concept Copyright © 2024
Derrick Charbonnet
Illustrations Copyright © 2024
Lala Bakir

THE INFORMATION IS PROVIDED "AS IS", WITHOUT WARRANTY OF ANY KIND, EXPRESS OR IMPLIED, INCLUDING, BUT NOT LIMITED TO THE WARRANTIES OF MERCHANTABILITY, FITNESS FOR A PARTICULAR PURPOSE AND NONINFRINGEMENT. IN NO EVENT SHALL THE AUTHORS OR COPYRIGHT HOLDERS BE LIABLE FOR ANY CLAIM, DAMAGES OR OTHER LIABILITY, WHETHER IN AN ACTION OF CONTRACT, TORT OR OTHERWISE, ARISING FROM, OUT OF OR IN CONNECTION WITH THE INFORMATION OR THE USE OR OTHER DEALINGS IN THE INFORMATION.

ISBN979-8-9890141-2-5

For Zhanay

Who asked the question.

And Kanat

Who encouraged me to write a book.

Please enjoy this book.

This is not a grammar book, good thing too,

since I am not a grammarian.

I do enjoy etymology:

words, and how they are used.

"Ass"

is probably the first swear word you used out loud. With the immediate defense: "It means **"Donkey!"**

So, what does it really mean?
Well, the rest of this book will tell you.

DONKEY!!!

> Well, it does mean donkey, but not exactly. The word seems to have come from the [African Wild Ass](), *Equus africanus*. These were domesticated a very long time ago and became common work animals.
>
> I don't know if this is part of history, but here is an interesting fact: an adult male donkey is usually called a *jack* or *jackass*.
>
> Know any adult males that could qualify for that name???
>
> An adult female donkey is a *jenny, but that name just doesn't have the same ring*.

But the word has an ass-load of other meanings and uses. I wrote this after a friend of mine asked about the meaning of "ass." English is not his first language, and he was very confused about the many ways he heard it used and wanted me to explain.

That explanation turned into this book!

Hopefully, you will enjoy this book and maybe learn a few new ways to use that multifaceted word! Please be sure to share this book with your friends from other countries. I'm quite sure they have questions and will have as much fun learning as we did.

There are other common uses of "ass" and this is where it starts getting interesting!

I try to avoid making this too much like a dictionary, but this book will use the following standards. The word or words will be in **BOLD**. After the word will be the explanation of the meaning. There may be a sentence with the word used as an example. Sentences need a subject, so I will use Jack and Jenny.

> NO!: All names, characters, and incidents portrayed in this production are fictitious. No identification with actual persons (living or deceased), places, buildings, and products is intended or should be inferred!

Be prepared! I suspect that since you are reading this book, you are prepared for a few swear words. Obviously, we use the word "ass" in this book. There are a few other "four letter" words in the text.

Time to start the lessons:

The first one is easy and certainly you are familiar with it:

ASS:
Quite literally your butt, your gluteus maximus, the thing you sit on, the thing you fall on.

> *I have a pimple on my ass.*
> *Jack tripped over the curb and fell on his ass.*

Now Jack doesn't actually have to land on his ass to "fall on his ass" it just has to be a spectacular fall.

This can also be used descriptively or sexually:

> *Jenny has a great ass.*

You can call someone an ass. It is a direct insult and questioning the other person's intelligence.

> *You're an ass.*
> *What an ass!*

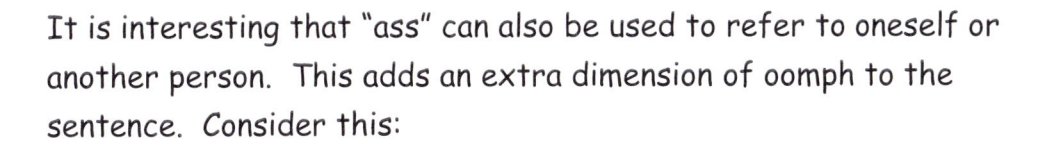

It is interesting that "ass" can also be used to refer to oneself or another person. This adds an extra dimension of oomph to the sentence. Consider this:

> *Get off my couch.*

Not much excitement there. So how about:

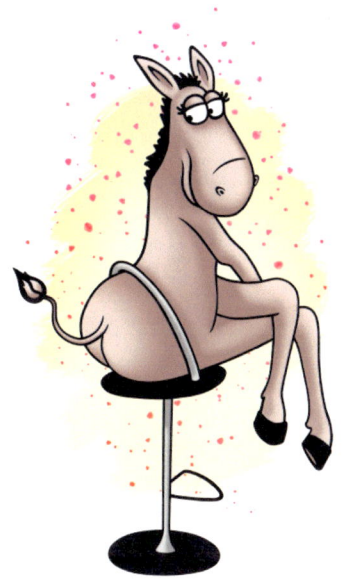

> *Get **your ass** off my couch.*

Much more punch!!!

It can also apply to you. Which is less likely to be confusing?

> *You can't get me on that roller coaster!*

or

> *You can't get my ass on that roller coaster!*

A couple of related words:

Asinine:
This is another related word. Basically stupid or like an ass (in the sense of a jerk)

> *This FB post is asinine, who would take it seriously.*

Asshole:
This is a very rude and very insulting thing to call someone. It is directly calling them a rectum, the least desirable part of an ass.

**Those are the simple and direct meanings.
The rest of this book:**

This wouldn't be a very interesting book if those were the only way ass is used. Fortunately for the funny bone in all of us, there are many, many more interesting and fascinating uses. The next section, Unique Uses, has the unique and special uses that make the word so interesting. Most of these combine the word "ass" with another word to make an entirely new word!

"Ass" can also be used just to emphasize another word, just like an exclamation point. The third part of the book, Emphatic, lists some of those common uses

Finally, we use ass in a wide range of strange and beautiful phrases. The fourth section of the book, Sayings and Sentences, teaches those.

Almost all of these uses are intended as humor or used as an insult. In a few cases, it can be used as a complement.

One more thing, the words are in no particular order.

Unique Uses:

My ass!

Yes, we used those words above, but these two words can also mean an emphatic "NO." Not sure why declaring "my ass" means no, but it clearly does!

> Jenny: "Jack, go clean up that mess!"
> Jack: "My ass!"

Haul ass

This is simple: to go fast.

> Jenny sure did haul ass when the hornets came out.

Ok, there is another version of this can be a pretty insulting and shaming. But I would not be fulfilling the obligation of this book if I didn't cover it:

> That dog is so fat, when it hauls ass, it has to make 2 trips!

Dumb-ass

This is usually just a general insult. But it doesn't just mean "stupid" it is more general insult to the person's character in addition to his intelligence.

> Wow, Jack is a dumb-ass, he can't do anything right.

It can also refer to individual acts or situations:

> That was a dumb-ass thing to do.

Smart-ass

This is NOT the opposite of dumb-ass. A smart-ass is not necessarily smart. A smart-ass has said or done something clever and annoying. It can be a general character reference.

> Jack is just a smart-ass; he is always annoying.

> Don't be a smart-ass, just get the work done.

Wise-ass

This is really just another way to say smart-ass.

> Jack always makes wise-ass comments.

This is not to be confused with the **Wise Ass On The Hill**. That is an "actual" donkey that is genuinely wise. He dispenses "wisdom" from a hill in one of my favorite comic strips.

Candy-ass
Wimpy or fragile.

> *That candy-ass kid is afraid to do anything.*

Kick ass, Kick his ass, Kick some ass. Kick ass and take names.
There are a lot of subtle meanings with this one. In its simplest meaning, it is to beat someone up. However, it is rarely used that way.

It more often is used to mean a big win or to obliterate an opponent in a game or sport.

> *Get out in that field and Kick ASS!*
>
> *Jack thought he was going to win that match, but I kicked his ass!*
>
> *Jenny looks like she is ready to go kick some ass.*
>
> *Alright boys, let's go kick ass and take names.*

"Kick ass and take names" is usually used when one or a few people are expected to beat a larger group, or just go and raise hell. To "take names" is a reference to putting people's names on a list to be punished.

Whup-ass, Open a can of whup-ass
This is similar to Kick Ass, but does usually mean physically overpowering someone. "Whup" is a slang version of "whip"

> *If Jack keeps annoying Jenny, she is going to whup his ass.*

To "Open a can of whup ass" is used to imply future action. It is simply a more interesting way to say you are going to beat someone up.

> *Jack looks angry, he's about to open up a can of Whup Ass.*

Bad-ass

This is a person who is tough and doesn't put up with anything. But can mean anyone that is supremely confident. (There is no expression "good-ass" just doesn't happen.)

> *Jack is a bad-ass, he has won every competition.*
>
> *Jenny looks like a bad-ass in that outfit.*
>
> *Don't' mess with him, he's a bad-ass and he won't put up with anything.*

Piece of ass

This is almost always a sexual reference and almost always a misogynistic way to refer to a woman.

> *That Jenny is a great piece of ass.*

In this case it is a reference to how good she looks and how much fun she could be in bed.

It can also be used to describe the sex act directly:

> *I got a great piece of ass last night.*

Ass-wipe

A completely useless person. Worse than useless. Not much else to say about this one. I'm pretty sure you can figure out where this comes from.

> *Jack is an ass-wipe, ignore him.*

Long-ass

This just means **really, really** long and outstanding. Sometimes used to express tiredness or being bored.

> *This has been a long ass trip.*
> *That is a long ass stick!*

Tight-ass

This has two very different meanings. The first is descriptive, a tight ass is someone's butt that is well shaped and has no flab.

> Jenny exercises a lot and has a tight ass.

The second meaning is a derogatory reference to someone who is cheap. This is a version of the much older insult "tight-wad"

> Jack is a tight ass.

Cheap-ass

This has two meanings. It can also be used to refer to someone who doesn't want to spend money.

> Jack is a cheap ass wood worker, he never buys new tools.

It can also be used to describe the quality of something. This is always derogatory.

> That is a cheap-ass phone,

Broke-ass

This has two meanings also. The first is just an insulting form of having no money.

> *Get your broke ass out of my apartment.*

The second describes something that is seriously broken or repeatedly broken.

> *That is one broke-ass car, I wouldn't go anywhere in it.*

Hard-ass, Cold-ass

This is someone with no emotion or empathy. Like your 10th grade phys-ed teacher.

> *Jack is a hard-ass, he doesn't care about anyone.*

Cold ass means the same thing.

Bust ass, Bust my ass
To work very hard.

> I'm going to have to really bust ass to finish on time.
> If I bust my ass, I can get it done today.
> You better be ready to bust your ass on this and get it done.

It can also mean that you were caught doing something and be punished.

> If Jack sees me doing this, he's gonna bust my ass.

Ass-kisser
This is a person that plays up to a boss, teacher, or someone in authority. Their intent is to get favorable treatment. They are generally disliked by others.

> Jenny is such as ass-kisser, I hate it when the boss cuts her some slack.

Kiss my ass

This is an expression of an unmitigated negative. Typically, it is not literal. It can be used several ways. It can be used as a rude way of saying no:

> Jack wanted me to help him move, I told him to "kiss my ass"

It can be used as a response to a comment that is disliked or to a situation as an indication that you are leaving.

> Jack: "You're ugly!" Jenny: "You can kiss my ass"
> I'm tired of this party, y'all can kiss my ass.

A variation of this is to "kiss your ass goodbye" which generally means your life is over (literally or figuratively).

> If Jack says he is going to beat you to a pulp, you can kiss your ass goodbye.

In rare cases, it is used as a positive sexual request.

Half-assed

Something that is very poorly done or incomplete is considered half-assed. It can also mean done with no enthusiasm or care, though the end result is pretty much the same thing.

> Jenny certainly did a half-assed job painting that room.

You might see public references to being "half fast." Don't let that fool you. When I was a little kid at a parade, I asked my Dad why the marching club was called the Half Fast Marching Club. I give him huge cred for keeping a totally straight face and telling me "maybe they walk slowly.

Ass load

A lot. **Really, really**, a lot of whatever you are referring to. Notice the similarity to "long-ass"

> Digging that pool was an ass-load of work.
> That is an ass-load of furniture on that truck.

Ass backwards (Bass ackwards)

This is just a more forceful way of saying something is the wrong way around. This can be used in a lot of different ways. A person or a thing can be ass backward. A tool or vehicle can be used ass backward. Someone can be putting something together ass backwards. Lots of ways!

> *Jack, I think you are using that tool ass backwards.*

The alternate "bass ackwards" is just a spoonerism that is less rude.

Red ass (a case of the red-ass)

If someone has a "case of the red-ass" it just means that they are irritated or angry. If you had a monumental case of diaper rash, you'd be pretty irritated AND angry.

> *Come back and talk to me when you get over your red-ass.*

Punk ass, Punk ass kid

This is used to insult someone and to imply they are young or inexperienced and think a bit much of themselves.

> *Leave me alone, you punk-assed-kid!*

Fat ass

It is typically used just to insult someone and to imply they are not doing something they are supposed to be doing. It can also mean really fat in a very insulting way.

> *Get your fat ass off the couch and repair the car.*

Lard ass

Basically, the same meaning as Fat Ass. Lard is rendered animal fat.

Sorry ass

This does not mean that you are sorry for doing something. It is an insult that means the person or thing is poor quality, weak, dumb, ignorant, or otherwise below standard.

> *That is one sorry-ass truck, it won't even change gears.*

In polite company the "ass" can be left off.

> *That is a sorry excuse for a truck.*

Emphatic:

The word ass can be added to **almost any other word** to just indicate special significance or just for emphasis. In these cases, it doesn't really change the meaning of the word.
Most of these must be used something like: "a *blank-ass something*".

Lazy ass
No real explanation needed.

> Jack is one lazy ass football player, why do they keep him on the team?

> Get your lazy ass away from the TV and get to work.

Big ass
This just means really big. This is now the Brand Name of a line of ceiling fans that are, well, really big.

Crazy ass
Someone who is really just not right.

> That crazy-ass Jenny jumped in the freezing mud puddle.

Hot ass, Cold ass
An extreme temperature, usually in an unpleasant way.

> I want a cold ass beer.
> That is a hot ass sidewalk, it started to melt my shoes

Stupid ass
If I have to explain this one...

Loud ass
Really, really loud.

> Those are loud ass speakers.

Bright ass

> Those are bright ass concert lights.

Tall ass, Short ass
Pretty simple, really tall or really short.

> Only tall ass people can play basketball.

Skinny ass
Yep, really skinny.

> That skinny assed dude was the only one that could climb that wall.

Grab ass
A vague sexual reference, someone that is unpleasant to be around. It can specifically refer to someone that gropes other people.

> I wish that grab ass would leave me alone.

There are many, many more.
Think of a word and add "ass"!!!

Sayings and Sentences:

This is where it gets fun and really interesting. We have so many expressions that mean so many things! How these came to be could be the subject of another book!!!

A Pain in my (the) ass
Something that is unpleasant to do or to be around. It can also be something or someone that is very irritating.

> *This detail work is a pain in the ass.*
>
> *Jack is a pain in my ass, I wish he would leave me alone.*

Stick it up your ass, Shove it up your ass
This is a complete and total rejection. Literally, it means take whatever is being offered an insert it (presumably painfully) where the sun doesn't shine.

> *I don't want that #$%@ thing. You can shove it up your ass for all I care.*
> *You can take this job and shove it!*

That one is a classic, even has its own country song. It is shortened for "politeness"

Don't let the door hit you on the ass on the way out.
This is a way to instruct someone to leave in a hurry. It means exactly what it says. Walk out the door quickly so that when it closes, it doesn't hit your ass! This can be because they need to hurry to some task, or you want them just to leave in a hurry.

Cover your ass
To do something or have paperwork that will protect you from unhappy consequences at some later time. It is often abbreviated as just CYA.

> Jack keeps a copy of the text from the boss just to cover his ass.
>
> Jenny let the boss know about the phone call just for CYA.

To work your ass off
Very simple. To work very hard. Your ass is still there, but I guess maybe it is smaller than when you started.

> Jenny worked her ass off getting the house clean.

Bite my ass

This is another way to clearly say "no" or to reject something.

> *If you think I'm going to give this to you, you can bite my ass.*

It's going to bite me in the ass
You say this when something is going to go wrong and it will turn out badly for you.

> *Jenny: Jacks lousy solution is going to come back and bite me in the ass*

Can't find his ass with both hands
This describes a person who is simply not the smartest person around.

> *Jenny is very nice, but she can't find her ass with both hands.*

If they are really far down the scale:

> *Jenny is very nice, but she can't find her ass with both hands in a well lit room.*

Your ass is grass
This is a way to say that you are going to lose badly, presumably being knocked down into the grass, though that isn't necessary. The rhyme is just fun.

> *If Jenny finds out you did this, your ass is grass.*

Knock you on your ass
Another threat or prediction that you are going to lose whatever interaction is coming up. This one is more explicit.

> *If you don't leave my motorcycle alone, I'm gonna knock you on your ass."*

Assume
This is a special one. The word "assume" is used when you don't know something for sure, but you use the thought anyway. This often leads to mistakes, missed meetings, and general embarrassment. There is a saying that wraps this up very neatly: To Assume is to make an "ass" of "u" and "me" (see the letters of "assume" there?)

> He assumed Jack and Jill were a couple because he saw them together. He was so embarrassed when he found out they weren't.

Pound sand up your ass
Another rejection. Also, an instruction to leave.

> Jack: "Want to take a tumble?"
> Jenny: "Go pound sand up your ass."

Assholes and elbows
When one or more people are working really hard or fast. Generally complementary. This has nothing to do with the actual work. But imagine a few people working a lot, perhaps digging, picking up things, or any activity that requires bending and grabbing things. If you are standing a bit away watching all the activity. What do you see?

> When Jack and Jenny really get to work, all you can see is assholes and elbows.

Blow it out of your ass
This is a lot like Bite My Ass. Pretty much another way to say no.

> Jenny: "I think you're ugly."
> Jack: "Blow it out your ass."

XXX out the ass, XXX coming out of my ass
A whole lot of anything. Substitute whatever there is a lot of for the XXX. This is neither good nor bad.

> She has cousins out the ass.
> That apartment has roaches out the ass.
> I just won a big bet and have money coming out my ass!

"...has a stick up their ass"
Generally, this refers to someone that walks very straight and stiffly.

> Jack walks like he has a stick up his ass.

It can also mean someone that is very boring and not fun.

Talking out of your ass

Totally making up whatever you are saying

> Jack: "blah blah blah blah blah"
> Jenny: "Shut up, Jack, you're just talking out of your ass"

To have your head up your ass
To be ignorant or totally unaware of what is going on.

> "Jack's gonna get fired. He's got his head up his ass and doesn't do anything right."

Horse's ass
A total jerk. This isn't really the ass that belongs to a horse, it is what you call someone who is acting like one.

> Jack is such a horse's ass.

Give a Rat's Ass
This saying is based on the assumption that the ass from a common rat is small and not very desirable. So, since it isn't very desirable, you would trade it for almost anything, Except, that is, for whatever the other person has.

> *I wouldn't give a rat's ass for that piece of junk.*

This also applies to other people's opinions.

> *Jenny: "I think your hair looks terrible"*
> *Jack: "I don't give a rat's ass what you think!"*

You can get a bit more colorful by saying "a white rat's ass."

Up someone's ass
Used when one person is continuously aggravating another person about something, typically about something they are supposed to do.

> *Jack has been up my ass all day, but I'm still not done,*

Blow smoke up someone's ass
This is to tell a lie or an attempt to confuse someone.

> Jenny is blowing smoke up my ass about the car she wants to sell. It is junk, but she says it is in good shape.

Wear my ass out
Doing something very physical that has made you tired.

> Mowing all these lawns is wearing my ass out.

Laugh my ass off, Laughing my ass off, LMAO
To find something very, very funny. So funny that your ass falls off. No, I don't know where this expression comes from.

> That picture was halarious, I laughed my ass off.

With their thumb up their ass

This is how you describe a person who is ignorant or uncoordinated and is trying to do something.

> *Jack has his thumb up his ass, he'll never get his car fixed.*

Drunk on their ass, drunk off their ass

Really, really, really drunk. Off and on are pretty interchangeable.

> *Jenny was drunk off her ass last night.*

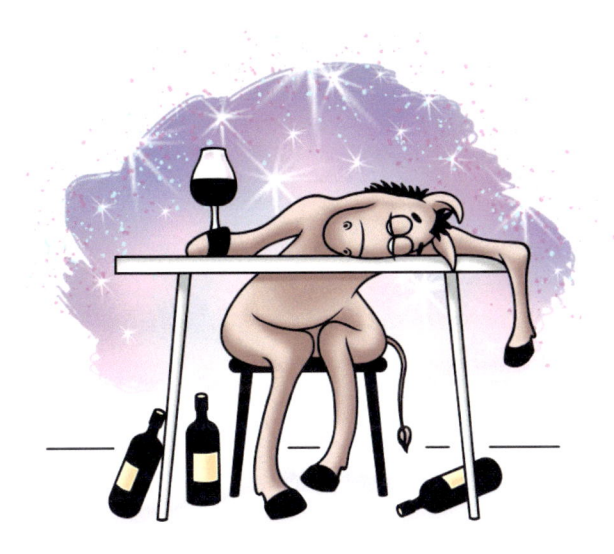

Pulled it out of my ass

To totally make up something.

> *Jenny doesn't have a clue, she pulled that number out of her ass.*

Doesn't know his ass from a hole in the ground

Someone who is very stupid. This is not subtle. If you can't tell the difference between these two things, you are pretty stupid indeed.

> What an idiot, Jack doesn't know his ass from a hole in the ground.

A related and much older saying is "he can't tell shit from Shinola." Shinola was a brand of shoe polish paste that came in a tin. Again, not very subtle.

Rip someone a new asshole

To tell someone that they have done a bad job. Done clearly and with no uncertainty. Usually, is done with many sentences not just a few words.

> Jenny's boss just ripped her a new asshole for losing that inventory.

To get my ass handed to me

To lose. To lose completely and totally. Completely humbled.

> I didn't even make 3rd place; I got my ass handed to me.

If your opponent is able to remove your ass and then before anything else happens, present it to you, then you have indeed been badly beaten.

A related expression to the hand someone their head on a platter. This comes from ancient history when the losers head was actually put on a stake for everyone to see.

Ass over teakettle

Somewhat old expression meaning to fall down. Usually falling down in a spectacular way. It has nothing to do with an actual teakettle.

It is related to the polite expression: "to fall head over heels." Although this expression usually associated with fall madly in love, I can't explain why if "your head is over your heels" that is something special. Neither can I explain how "Ass over Teakettle" came from "Head over heels".

> *Jack slipped, dropped the tray of drinks, and fell ass over teakettle.*

Ass Cap

A tattoo located just above a woman's buttocks. Males rarely have a tattoo in this spot. Also called a Tramp Stamp. Generally derogatory.

Asshole drinking buddy

This is a person that you regularly meet at a bar to laugh too loud and be rude. That person isn't a real friend, just a drinking buddy. Worse, when you are with this drinking buddy, you both act like jerks.

> *Jenny and Jack aren't dating, they are just asshole drinking buddies.*

Crawling up my ass

This one is pretty specific. When you are driving and someone is tailgating very, very closely and doesn't back off or change lanes, that person is "crawling up your ass."

Bare ass naked

This is exactly what is says. Someone has no clothes on (maybe shoes). Typically, this would be used to describe a very embarrassing situation.

> When her tent blew over, there she was, bare assed naked.

Underwear bunched up

The "ass" is implied here and it is very similar to a case of the red ass. If someone is irritated and grumpy, they could have their underwear all bunched up and be very uncomfortable. An alternate and much older version is "his knickers are in a knot."

Sit on it and rotate

The "ass" is implied here, too. It is an instruction as well as an insult and a rejection. The "it" can be anything in your imagination, the implication is that whatever "it" is, once you sit on it, you will be positioned to rotate round on it.

> Jack: "Hey baby, want some of this?"
> Jenny: "Sit on it and rotate!"

Your ass sucks wind

I have no explanation for this one, but it is a general insult.

> Jenny: Jack, you're ugly and dress funny.
> Jack: Your ass sucks wind.

Have one we missed? Email us at:

Ass@ItMeansDonkey.com

By sending me a suggestion (OR ANYTHING), you give me the right to use it. I will try to credit you when possible, but if many people send in the same thing then it is public domain.

Made in the USA
Columbia, SC
07 November 2024